Aiming Higher: Universities and Australia's future

First published in 2025 by Australia Institute Press
Reprinted in 2025

ISBN 978-1-7636621-7-9 (print)
ISBN 978-1-7636621-8-6 (ebook)

Published in Australia and New Zealand by
Australia Institute Press
www.australiainstitute.org.au

Cataloguing-in-publication data is available from the National Library of Australia

Copyedited by Rod Morrison

Printed and bound in Australia by McPherson's Printing Group, an accredited ISO AS/NZS 14001 Environmental Management Systems printer.

Aiming Higher: Universities and Australia's future

George Williams

Australia Institute Press

A system under strain

Welcome Week to herald the start of semester at Western Sydney University in 2025 was packed with excited students keen to make friends and begin their academic journey. There was, however, one difference from other years. Students not only queued to join clubs and societies; they also sought handouts of food.

Students around the nation are struggling to make ends meet. For many, university is a time of poverty. Half of our students at Western have food insecurity, with many missing meals. Unsurprisingly, they struggle to finish their studies, with those from poorer backgrounds increasingly quitting or not going to university at all.

Too often, being a university student means going hungry.

We responded by opening a Western Pantry

on our Kingswood campus in Penrith in mid-2024. It provides free staples like rice, oats and pasta. The demand has proved to be enormous, with 3,400 visits in the second half of 2024. We have since opened another pantry in Parramatta and pop-up pantries on other campuses and will also provide more than 23,000 free dinners and breakfasts in 2025.

As I handed out food to the 100 or more students who came to our Pantry during Welcome Week, I asked them why they were there. The Youth Allowance payment of $47 a day for students who cannot live at home does not cover the rent, let alone food, transport, medicine and textbooks. They spoke about the Pantry being the difference between staying in university or dropping out.

Sadly, shortages of food and other basics, combined with unreasonably high university fees, have become the reality of higher education today for many students. The system is failing them. As older generations accumulate increasing amounts of wealth through property, tax concessions and other investments, our youth are struggling to get ahead and face the prospect of being locked out of housing.

It was not like this for previous generations. Fresh out of high school in the 1980s, I knew that university was a pathway to opportunity. The system was structured in a way that if I worked hard and took advantage of what higher education provided, I could expect a well-paid job, a great career and the best that life in Australia could offer. Higher education reflected the egalitarian ideal that everyone deserves "a fair go".

This is still true today for students from well-off backgrounds, but often not for others. For them the social compact is broken. Those who would benefit most from a university education are frequently the least able to afford it. The system does not provide a ladder of opportunity for everyone. Our modern institutions are simply too expensive and too difficult to navigate and, as a result, many people are missing out on the social mobility that higher education offers.

The ladder to a better life is missing more than a few rungs.

The issue of student poverty in Australia rarely enters the public debate when it comes to our universities. The interests of those whom the system should serve — students and the community — too often take a backseat to public concern over unpaid wages, sexual assaults on campuses, anti-Semitism and freedom of speech, and the perennial issue of executive pay.

As these issues dominate the agenda, it is easy to lose sight of the mission of our universities and the public good they deliver. The debate also obscures the larger role of higher education. Universities are a central part of our civic life as anchor institutions in their local communities and underpin the success of our democracy. Our economic and social progress depends upon their success as generators of knowledge, creativity, invention and social mobility. If you want to change the world for the better, education is the place to start.

But something has gone badly wrong. Anger at universities, with escalating concerns about governance and intense political pressure from all sides, have left universities friendless and alone. And when universities lose, it is not just students who suffer, it is the nation at large.

This is not a recent phenomenon. The well-being of our universities has deteriorated over decades and has reached a tipping point where the financial sustainability of many institutions is under threat. The plight of the sector mirrors the strains of modern Australia, with some universities under dire financial pressure while others record large profits. The media narrative alternates between job losses and excessive executive pay.

Today, universities find themselves in the distressing position where their very social licence is in question. An increasingly hostile media and uninterested public, combined with a host of inquiries and a growing thicket of regulation that challenge the autonomy and mission of our universities, have created a perfect storm.

Universities have become the political equivalent of the banking sector before the 2017 Hayne Royal Commission. With the way things are going, it is hard to rule out the prospect of a similar inquiry into the nation's universities.

The plight of universities can be seen daily in the media, including in outlets that had been sympathetic. On 28 June 2025 *The Sydney Morning Herald* ran a story under the headline "'A kind of monster': why does everyone hate universities?".[1] The headline and article attracted a lot of discussion, but nobody I spoke to doubted the premise of the question.

A few days later, columnist Jenna Price unloaded on universities in the same newspaper in a piece entitled "Don't go to university next year. Just don't". She wrote:

> Going to university in 2026 is a risk no-one should take. Universities are now places of chaotic cost-cutting and cruel managers whose sole interest is the bottom line. Entire disciplines are being cut, staff numbers slashed and there is an even greater than usual reliance on casual staff who are, appropriating Beyonce's poeticism, underpaid and overwhelmed.[2]

When friends of the sector are publicly dishing out such strong criticism, it is reckless to ignore it. To say community sentiment is at a low ebb would be generous. Years of negative press and scandals have led Australians to question whether universities are prioritising surpluses over students.

A YouGov poll for The Australia Institute in June 2025 found 80 per cent of those surveyed agreed that the primary purpose of universities should be educating students, with only 3 per cent saying it should be making a profit.[3] On the other hand, when people were asked about the primary purpose of universities *currently*, the most popular answer was making a profit at 54 per cent, with educating students at 44 per cent.

This contrast in the public mind between mission and performance runs in tandem with a loss of public trust. A poll in early 2024 showed that a majority of Australians no longer have a positive view of their universities. Most (52 per cent) were either neutral or negative, demonstrating a massive slide in confidence.[4]

This reflects a worldwide trend, exemplified by a catastrophic fall of support in the United States. In that country the percentage of people expressing "a great deal" or "quite a lot" of confidence in universities dropped from 57 per cent in 2015 to 36 per cent in 2024, while those with little or no confidence increased from 10 per cent to 32 per cent — and these figures were before the re-election of President Donald Trump and his assault on American universities.[5]

But as public opinion has soured, too often our universities have downplayed the issues or painted themselves as cash-strapped victims. This has not gone down well with political leaders or the public who instead see a counter-narrative of surpluses and vice-chancellors paid better than prime ministers and premiers. The way universities have responded to their loss of social licence has itself contributed to the downward spiral, reinforcing public concern that the sector has lost its way.

Reversing the situation to regain public trust is not something that government can impose. Successive waves of regulation have demonstrated that the heavier the government's hand, the greater the unintended consequences of reform.

Now is the time for a different type of revolution. Now is the time for universities to reconnect with those they serve: students and the community. This should be our singular focus as we take action to remedy the situation.

Losing our way

Universities as repositories of knowledge and learning have existed for nearly a thousand years, well before many of the institutions that define our democracy. The first university was established in the Italian city of Bologna in 1088. In Australia, the University of Sydney was created 175 years ago, modelled on the elite institutions of London, Cambridge and Oxford.

The evolution of Australian universities has passed through three distinct phases. These were first defined by Dr Hannah Forsyth and paraphrased by Professor John Quiggin as: the sandstone era from 1850 to 1945 that saw each state establish its own university; the era of expansion from 1945 to the election of the Hawke Labor government in 1983; and the era of transformation from the 1980s to today.[6]

The post-World War II era of expansion saw the Commonwealth take over primary funding for universities, while leaving the states in charge of governance. This split responsibility continues to the present day as a source of regulatory incoherence.

This era of sweeping social and economic change saw the Whitlam Labor government in 1974 introduce free university education. Ahead of the 1972 election in his "It's Time" speech, Whitlam declared:

> We will abolish fees at universities and colleges of advanced education. We believe that a student's merit rather than a parent's wealth should decide who should benefit from the community's vast financial commitment to tertiary education. And more, it's time to strike a blow for the ideal that education should be free.

For many, Whitlam's 1974 reforms remain the high water mark. But while university education was free of charge, it was not freely available. Limited places meant that problems of equity and access remained.

Dawkins reforms

The Dawkins reforms in the 1980s, named for Education Minister John Dawkins in the Hawke Labor government, remade Australia's higher education sector. In many ways, the basic structure and market orientation that he put in place remain intact, including incentives for universities to compete internationally and operate like corporate entities.

Competition between universities and their embrace of a profit motive has suited successive governments. It has meant that universities increasingly raise revenue from market-based sources, including student fees, rather than relying on the public purse. In 1995 the federal government spent 0.9 per cent of GDP on universities, with this dropping a third to 0.6 per cent in 2021 (implying a $6.5 billion reduction).[7] To put it another way, in the 1980s the federal government contributed around 80 per cent of the sector's funding, now it is closer to 40 per cent[8] while the number of students has more than tripled to over 1.6 million.

Dawkins increased the size of the sector, which opened up access and led to a more than doubling of the percentage of Australians who study at university (from two in ten to four in ten people today).[9] He did so by transforming colleges of advanced education and institutes of technology into universities. In 1989 the University of Western Sydney (now Western Sydney University) was founded as a federated network university through an amalgamation of the Nepean College of Advanced Education, Hawkesbury Agricultural College and Macarthur Institute of Higher Education. Similar transformations took place around the country.

Dawkins and Hawke built a system that fused Labor's aspiration for fairness and equality with their own stamp of economic rationalism that was then very much in vogue. Government policies included floating the Australian dollar to integrate the Australian economy with global markets, allowing foreign banks into Australia, reducing tariffs, and privatising or corporatising government-owned enterprises such as QANTAS, Telecom (now Telstra) and the Commonwealth Bank. University policy directed towards corporatisation and competing in international markets was yet another example.

In a world first, the Hawke government introduced the income contingent Higher Education Contribution Scheme (HECS) in 1989. University students were charged $1,800 a year, regardless of the course they were studying. Repayments, at 1 per cent of income, started once their pay reached $22,000, rising to 2 per cent at $25,000.[10]

Domestic enrolments soared and lecture halls heaved as the system welcomed thousands of new students, many of them the first in their family to attend university.

My entry to university in 1987 was part of this era, at the suburban Macquarie University in Sydney. Early on in my life, coming from a single-parent family, I did not anticipate that university was for me. Studying economics and law opened up new opportunities and set me on a path that would have been unattainable otherwise. Like so many other Australians back then, university meant social mobility and a chance at a better life.

It is why I am so determined that a child's postcode and the circumstances of their parents should not dictate their future. Education changed my life, and I believe every person should have the same opportunity.

During the Dawkins era of rapid growth, the Hawke government introduced a full-fee-paying system for international students. Higher education expert Professor Andrew Norton from Monash Business School described it as one of the most important higher-education policy decisions ever made: "Public universities proved to be surprisingly entrepreneurial, sparking double-digit annual international enrolment growth rates through the 1990s."[11]

The nation's universities thrived among international competition, becoming the envy of many other nations in their ability to attract the best and brightest from around the world. In 2024 international students made up 26 per cent of total enrolments in Australian universities.[12]

The shift to attract international students had many flow-on effects, including Australian universities increasingly playing the international rankings game. These are scored by organisations such as QS and Times Higher Education with universities vying to become one of the top 200, 100 or even 50 universities in the world. The scoring is weighted in favour of research over student satisfaction, leading universities to prioritise the former while the latter has eroded.

Australia has achieved remarkable success in international university rankings. In the 2026 QS rankings, for example, Australia has nine universities in the top 100, more than any other nation except the United States and the United Kingdom. And on a per capita basis Australia far exceeds those nations. When it comes to university rankings, Australia outperforms the world. This matters not just for bragging rights or prestige, but because rankings are a key attractor of international students.

This has produced a self-reinforcing cycle. Universities prioritise research, which boosts their rankings, thereby attracting more international students, whose course fees provide the income to fund research, and so on. Notably, the education of Australian students does not fit within this dynamic; at best, they are cross-subsidised by the additional income from their international counterparts. The system incentivised this as government funding declined, especially so for major universities able to compete on the world stage.

The Dawkins reforms sowed the seeds for decades of over-reliance on international students and the revenue they generate. They also propelled universities down an increasingly corporatised path. As the editors of the 2013 book, *The Dawkins Revolution, 25 Years On*, put it:

> Dawkins … turned colleges into universities, free education into HECS, elite education into mass education, local focuses into international outlooks, vice-chancellors into corporate leaders … He remodelled higher education and how it was funded in only a few years.[13]

Such radical change has had many unintended consequences with which governments have been grappling ever since. A change of government in 1996 brought new policies under Liberal Prime Minister John Howard. This included replacing the single course fee under HECS with differential course fees, whereby students able to earn higher salaries on graduation (in areas such as business and law) were charged more.

The sector underwent significant reform again in 2012, with the Gillard Labor government scrapping capped student places to usher in the demand-driven system recommended by the 2008 Bradley Review. Universities could enrol unlimited numbers of Australian bachelor-degree students into any discipline other than medicine and be paid for each of them.[14] The number of bachelor-degree students soared but the system groaned under the expense. As Professor Andrew Norton observed:

> The policy ended because of cost. By 2017, demand-driven funding had caused spending to increase by more than 50% in real terms since 2008. From 2013 to 2017, every federal budget included an attempt to curb higher education spending, while keeping the demand-driven system.[15]

The Turnbull Coalition government ultimately responded by freezing bachelor-degree spending.

$50,000 arts degrees

The system veered off the rails in 2021 with the introduction of the Morrison Coalition government's Job-ready Graduates (JRG) Package. This blunt, ill-conceived policy removed the link introduced by the Howard government between student fees and graduate earnings in favour of setting prices based upon what the government wanted students to study. The idea was that a strong price signal would steer students away from the arts and humanities into areas of national labour shortage such as mathematics, agriculture and nursing. It took the idea of a market for higher education to an entirely new level, distancing the system even further from the notion of education as a public good.

The policy failed in its own terms and also failed the nation as a whole. While the plan was, for example, to use high prices for arts degrees and low prices for agriculture degrees to change student choices, it was based on a fundamental misunderstanding of how students choose what to study. A potential history student did not seek a career in farming, nor did a student passionate about philosophy shift to mathematics. Instead, it made the entire university system more socially regressive and inequitable.

Price has not proved to be a significant determinant of choice between degrees. One study found that fewer than one in fifty students changed their field of study due to differential fees.[16] But while price has little impact on what degree to enrol in, the cost of a young person's preferred degree can have a life-defining influence on whether they study or not. Not only are students now lumbered with higher fees and debt, but many are dissuaded from going to university at all.

The JRG introduced deep unfairness. Arts degrees covering areas such as history and English literature moved to the highest fee category with business and law, despite arts graduates earning the lowest graduate incomes and often coming from the most disadvantaged parts of society. An arts student incurs a debt of $16,992 per year or $50,976 for three years of study, compared with $4,627 a year or $13,881 for three-year degrees in areas including agriculture, statistics and mathematics. The prices will increase further in 2026. Many arts graduates never earn enough to pay this off because of their low salaries and the ongoing indexation of their debt, effectively incurring a debt until death.

The annual cost of an arts degree is now nine times the original 1989 contribution, a rate well ahead of inflation. Student fees have increased from a third of the salary earned by an arts student on graduation to more than two-thirds.[17]

Australians think that students are being asked to pay far too much for their degrees. Just under half (47 per cent) of Australians surveyed by YouGov in June 2025[18] believe that a worker on an average income should be able to pay off the debt for a standard three-year degree within five years. Just under one in five, or 18 per cent, believe a standard degree should be free. When it comes to the cost of a degree, 58 per cent believe a student should pay $5,000 or less per year, less than a third of what arts students now pay.

Extracting more fees from students has led to student debt reaching astronomical levels. It peaked at more than $81 billion before the Albanese Labor government reduced debts by 20 per cent and shaved $16 billion off the total.

It says much about the nation's priorities that each year the government collects far more from student debt repayments than it does from the gas industry through the Petroleum Resource Rent Tax ($5.1 billion as opposed to $1.1 billion in 2023–2024).[19] Unsurprisingly, the Universities Admissions Centre found that concern over HECS debt influences the decision to attend university for 40 per cent of Year 12 students.[20]

Record high fees and the associated debt is only one of the major pressures faced by Australian students. Like the rest of the community, they have also been hit by cost-of-living pressures that have left many in poverty. As a result, the proportion of students having to support full-time study with full-time work has doubled from one in fourteen students in the 1990s to one in seven in 2023.[21] This mix is devastating for students and causes many to drop out. Full-time work *or* full-time study is difficult enough, let alone trying to combine the two.

Big increases by university students in part- and full-time work mean that many have little time for campus life and can miss out on the best that university has to offer. Work pressures can force them to treat study as a fly-in, fly-out experience. Unsurprisingly, campus attendance is down, as is participation in university life. I often talk to students at Western about this, and many have told me how hard it is to make friends and how they feel lonely. They are also missing out on making new connections and joining networks that can break down the social barriers that increasingly define Australian society.

Students are taking longer to pay off their debt, now taking 9.9 years on average compared to 7.3 years in 2006.[22] Government policies that permit delaying repayment to higher income levels will further slow this, meaning that many graduates will hold student debt well into their thirties as they face other financial challenges, such as securing a home loan or starting a family.

The Albanese government's one-off decision to wipe 20 per cent off student debt will cut $5,520 from the average graduate debt of $27,600. This makes a meaningful difference for graduates yet to pay off their debt, but it does nothing to address the problem with the level of the fees in the first place. In particular, the policy provides no benefits to new students. It is akin to addressing the housing crisis by paying off 20 per cent of every current mortgage without doing anything to reduce the cost of housing.

The deep problems with student fees are well known. The interim report of the Australian Universities Accord, released in June 2023, said the JRG package needs to be fixed "before it causes long-term and entrenched damage" and that without change the higher education system "will rapidly become unfit for purpose".[23] New students will be saddled with the consequences of the JRG for the long term. Every day we delay a fix is a bad day for the current cohort of students.

The Productivity Commission joined the call for a "new funding model as a priority" given the "design flaws" of the JRG. It said the "differences in student contributions by perceived labour market needs fail to meet their goals while arbitrarily increasing debt burdens on some students".[24] The Accord's final report in February 2024 highlighting this unfairness found the student fee structure needs to be replaced.

The government has yet to act on this and instead students must wait for the newly established Australian Tertiary Education Commission to design a new funding and fees model.

Australian Universities Accord

The predicament of higher education has worsened under the watch of several governments. It is not something the current government has managed to turn around. Federal Education Minister Jason Clare began with ambition and promise when he announced a plan in November 2022 to develop the Accord. This was billed as the first broad review of the higher education system for nearly 15 years. It was "an opportunity to look at everything from funding and access, to affordability, transparency, regulation, employment conditions and how higher education and vocational education and training can and should work together".[25]

With the stage set for a generational shake-up of post-secondary learning, hopes were high. The interim Accord report recognised, in the words of higher education expert Professor Graeme Turner, that the system is "broken".[26] It described the need for "system wide change" and that this "must get underway as soon as possible".[27]

The Accord's final report set out a blueprint for decades-long change, including opening higher education to the broadest possible group to enable 80 per cent of working-age

Australians to be tertiary educated by 2050, up from 60 per cent today. Achieving this would add $240 billion in additional income to the economy over that period.[28]

The Albanese government has implemented important aspects of the Accord, including a National Student Ombudsman, paid placements for teaching, nursing, social work and midwifery students (so students receive financial support while they complete the intensive, mandatory parts of their program), and regional and suburban study hubs. It was quick to scrap the rule that required bachelor-degree students to maintain a pass rate of at least 50 per cent after eight units to remain eligible to receive Commonwealth assistance. The government also expanded demand-driven funding to all Indigenous students.

On the other hand, the Accord continues to struggle under the weight of its 47 recommendations, many of which are unfunded. Other aspects of the Accord have been overtaken by policies from left field that were not in the document. The most significant was the government's 2024 decision to cap the number of international students who can enter Australia to preserve housing for Australians. In removing billions of dollars of future revenue from the sector, many institutions were left in financial crisis, less able to serve the needs of Australian students and conduct research.

The government has not addressed the most fundamental aspects of the Accord. The broken JRG pricing and funding system remains in place. As a result, the system remains rife with perverse incentives that encourage corporatisation and the pursuit of rankings over student success. Universities must take responsibility for their own failings, but it is also fair to say that many of these are a product of governments steering universities in the wrong direction.

The new "boat people"

Of all the Albanese government's changes, the most seismic was the reversal of Australia's attitude to international students. International students contribute more than $50 billion to the national economy each year and were responsible for more than half of Australia's economic growth in 2023.[29] Education is the nation's second largest export after resource extraction.[30] After decades of encouraging, indeed incentivising, universities to enrol international students the government slammed on the brakes in 2024.

Within the space of a few months, measures were introduced that fundamentally altered Australia's engagement with international education. This included risk-based processing of visas that led to longer wait times. The government also sent a dramatic price signal by more than doubling the international student visa application fee from $710 to $1,600, increasing it again to $2,000 from 1 July 2025. This is five to ten times higher than the fee charged by many other comparable countries and is non-refundable, meaning that a student does not get their money back if their visa is not processed or denied.

Some students from countries such as China are able to pay higher visa fees. On the other hand, consider a student from the Philippines or Nepal looking to study nursing. It is less likely that this student, often supported by their family's life savings, will apply to study in Australia.

The result is a signal to universities to move away from diversification across price-sensitive markets in Southeast Asia in favour of increasing dependence on students from China. This is at odds with the government's Southeast Asia economic strategy, which states: "Australia's education sector is a national asset in our engagement with Southeast Asia. It has been integral to building enduring relationships and economic prosperity with the region".[31]

International students generate enormous levels of goodwill towards Australia. They often become political leaders and champions of business after their return to their home country. Alumni of Australian universities include Dr Boediono, former vice president of Indonesia; Dr Marty Natalegawa, former foreign minister of Indonesia; Akhilesh Yadav, an Indian politician who served as chief minister of Uttar Pradesh; and Malaysian businessman Dr Cheong Choong Kong, former CEO of Singapore Airlines, to name but a few.

Australia will miss out on the full benefits that international education can bring by restricting the ability of students from Southeast Asia to study here. It says a lot about our nation's priorities that no one would consider curbing our iron ore exports, and yet our largest export industry that does not involve digging something up from the ground and which benefits peace and security in our region has been restricted.

It is unconscionable that we treat our regional neighbours this way. Their families pool their wealth to enable a child to study in Australia as a pathway to a better life, and we charge them an exorbitant fee to be trapped in what can be a long visa processing queue with no refund if they are not granted a visa. The cruel impact upon students left anxious and distressed does not speak well of us as a welcoming country. It also makes Australia a far less attractive place to study. That, of course, is the point of the policy.

The government took a further step by announcing it would restrict net overseas migration from 528,000 in 2022–2023 to 260,000 by 2025–2026. Restricting the number of international students entering Australia was the focus of this policy. The government justified it on the basis that it was required to safeguard housing for Australians. Then Opposition Leader Peter Dutton went so far as to label international students seeking to extend their stay in Australia as "the modern version of boat arrivals".[32]

The government sought to enforce a cap on international students through legislation. When this was not passed by Parliament, the government responded by introducing a ministerial direction that had the same effect. The direction lists the total number of visas provided for study at each university, with the Department of Home Affairs processing the first 80 per cent of those in a first come, first served basis and then working through the remainder when they have the time.

Limiting the number of international students able to enter Australia ran counter to decades of higher education policy. It also ran counter to the financial model underpinning the sector. As federal governments progressively withdrew funding from universities, they came to increasingly rely on international student revenue to cross-subsidise essential activities. For the nation's oldest universities, this supported research. For newer universities, the cross-subsidisation supported Australian students from poorer backgrounds.

The international student cap was introduced in haste and has led to unintended consequences, including spillover effects for Australian students. At Western Sydney University, we spend 24 cents of every dollar we receive from international students on services such as food and academic support programs for Australian students.

We also have a bed for every international student who wants one. We even have spare capacity of around 25 per cent in our purpose-built accommodation. Our international students enrich our local communities and with their families account for a large share of tourism in New South Wales. Many also work in local businesses, with one local pizza shop owner reporting that international students make all of his pizzas — and buy 70 per cent of them.

Another unintended consequence of the

hardline stance has been to dissuade and limit people who want to come to Australia to study nursing. These are students that the government hopes will stay in Australia after completing their degree to help alleviate our shortage of health professionals. In Western Sydney alone, there is a deficit of some 10,000 nurses, in good part because insufficient numbers of Australian students are choosing to study this field. Government policy means that the international students who could help fill this gap are prevented from entering the country, leaving the government to instead pay a premium to attract fully trained nurses from elsewhere.

Government policy on international students is unlikely to make a significant difference to the nation's housing problems. That complex issue goes back many years and has very little to do with international students. It is also based on the misconception that international students are wealthy and taking homes from Australians. The reality is very different. For many, the journey to our shores requires the combined sacrifice of an entire family. At Western Sydney University, we see this truth every day.

Many of our international students from

countries such as Nepal, Vietnam and India are doing it tough. They are balancing study, part-time work and loneliness, all in the hope of improving their future. They are also hit by cost-of-living pressures, with many going hungry. International students are frequent users of our food pantries.

International students are not coming to Sydney and purchasing million-dollar homes in places like Parramatta. They live in student accommodation, share houses or board with friends. Many live with local families through a homestay program. This provides around $400 a week to help with mortgage and other cost-of-living pressures. The family in return provides a safe and caring environment.

The Albanese government undercut the vision that Dawkins and Hawke had for international education, and indeed of a nation that is outward-looking and globally competitive. Returning to a "fortress Australia" mentality similar to that during the COVID-19 pandemic sends the wrong signal at home and abroad about our willingness to engage with the world.

The government's changes have a major financial effect on the nation's universities that receive billions of dollars of revenue each year from international students. There is no doubting their dependence, with universities on average receiving about a quarter of their revenue (and some over 40 per cent) from international student fees. Many Australian jobs depend on this as it has proved to be the only source of growth sufficient to alleviate the decline in government funding. Upturning a system that has been shaped by decades of government policy within a matter of months has resulted in extreme financial stress for some universities and the loss of thousands of jobs.

Deficits, compliance and risk

Australia's 39 public universities educate more than 1.6 million local and international students and employ over 137,000 people. We are a rich country but, like a large percentage of our students, many of our universities are cash-strapped. In 2023 two-thirds were in deficit. The situation improved in 2024, with large surpluses in some universities such as $545 million at the University of Sydney and $204 million at the University of New South Wales, but other universities experienced another year of loss. In New South Wales many reported deficits, with the Auditor-General warning that six had less than three months of cash reserves, which "may signal financial sustainability risk".[33]

Australia has a two-track higher education system divided between those students who can afford to study at university and those who cannot, and universities with large surpluses and those that are cutting jobs. The division is even more problematic because it is typically universities in the midst of the greatest financial stress and cutting jobs that also cater to students from the poorest backgrounds.

International student caps are the most

recent driver of the financial problems of universities, but the causes go back much further, thanks to declining funding. Real funding for Commonwealth-supported students has fallen by $2 billion since 2020, with average funding for each Commonwealth-supported student falling 8 per cent between 2013 and 2023.[34]

The Morrison government's JRG package has made things much worse. In its first year in 2021, students paid an estimated $414 million in additional fees, an average increase of 8 per cent. At the same time, universities received $1 billion less in Commonwealth Grant Scheme funding, a 15 per cent decline.[35] Universities were forced to do more with less, putting pressure on their budgets, and further exacerbating the problem of unacceptably high levels of casual employment (with around half of all teaching across the sector now delivered by people on short-term contracts[36]).

While universities have progressively received less funding to teach each Australian student, the cost of educating these students has risen. In February 2025 analysis by Times Higher Education found the cost rose by more than one-fifth in just four years.[37]

Commonwealth funding for universities is based on Equivalent Full-Time Student Load (EFTSL). This means that universities receive the same funding for educating one student full-time as they do for two students each studying part-time. The problem with this is that the latter can cost more, in part since the support needs and demand for services of two students can be more expensive than one, especially where the students are from disadvantaged backgrounds or have special needs. Our food pantries do not give half the amount of food to a part-time student compared to one studying full-time.

The increase in part-time students has created an imbalance in the "cost to serve" students. Consultancy firm KordaMentha found the sector's cost to serve rose 22 per cent between 2018 and 2022 which again puts pressure on the financial position of universities.[38]

Inflation has also driven up costs, with KordaMentha finding staff costs rose 12 per cent between 2019 and 2023. Spending on things such as security, travel, marketing, scholarships, maintenance and consumables increased 16 per cent, according to universities' annual reports. Expanded compliance costs, the use of consultants and executive pay also added to these expenses. Another major factor has also been the rising cost of conducting medical and other research.

The discussion about corporatisation often overlooks the context in which universities must operate. The cost to comply with government rules and regulations has been particularly expensive. For example, New South Wales universities have to navigate 331 Commonwealth and state laws. Many of these are important and some determine safety standards. On the other hand, too many impose unnecessary layers of regulation and bureaucracy that mean salaries which would otherwise go to teachers and researchers are diverted to professional staff wading through red tape and ticking boxes.

Selling out the generational bargain

Too often, Australian students have suffered due to the pressures facing universities. Students today are paying much more but getting less than their predecessors.

The current system is geared against Australian students. The need to remedy government funding shortfalls has led many universities to prioritise international student recruitment. Discretionary funds have often been used not to enhance the student experience but to bolster research performance, as this drives rankings that help to attract more international students.

In a market-driven system where universities need to raise additional revenue, Australian students, with declining federal funding, can be a second-order priority. Students at some universities have complained about how their experience in the classroom is affected by increases in the number of international students in courses such as commerce and business. Australian students can find themselves in classes dominated by overseas students, particularly from China, with varying levels of spoken and written English. The result can be unsatisfactory both for domestic students and for those from overseas seeking an Australian experience rather than a classroom dominated by peers from their home country.

Even while Australian universities have achieved extraordinary, world-leading research outcomes and remarkable rankings success, many students remain dissatisfied with their education. Government policy and market pressures have redefined what success means for many Australian universities, and this in turn has eroded their core mission of educating students.

The most recent data from the Quality Indicators for Learning and Teaching (QILT) on the annual Student Experience Survey (SES) presents a problematic picture.[39] In 2023 undergraduate student ratings of satisfaction with the quality of the educational experience were 76.7 per cent across the sector. Postgraduate coursework satisfaction sat at 77.1 per cent. The figures show that nearly one in four students is dissatisfied. There are not many organisations that can sustain such levels of unhappiness for an extended period.

The survey also revealed the pressures felt by students. Almost one in five undergraduates, or 18.7 per cent, considered leaving in 2023, with stress levels and financial difficulties ranked as the top reasons. Less than half of undergraduate and postgraduate coursework students had a positive sense of belonging to their institution.

Surely, this should ring alarm bells. How can we better serve students when so many lack connection with us? Indeed, many are bypassing university altogether. Applications and offers for domestic undergraduates sit at around the same levels as 2012, despite a 20 per cent increase in the Australian population over that period — indicating a significant decline in the proportion of Australians willing to sign up for an undergraduate degree.[40]

It is not just universities struggling with engagement and outcomes.

Australia's entire education system is in danger of selling out the generational bargain, failing to ensure that those who come after us are better off. There is something deeply wrong with the trajectory of our education system.

We know the years before a child turns five are instrumental in their development, and it is pleasing to see a collective focus on the importance of early childhood learning. The Albanese government's commitment to build a universal early childhood education and care system where every child who needs it is eligible for at least three days per week of subsidised early education and care is laudable. It is a downpayment on ensuring all children have a good start to their education journey.

Work to ensure childcare is safe, affordable and accessible remains incomplete, especially in areas such as Sydney's west where "childcare deserts" persist and places close to home, work and transport options can be hard to come by.

Once children reach primary school, the National Assessment Program — Literacy and Numeracy (NAPLAN) assesses them in Years 3, 5, 7 and 9. In 2025 the results showed that nearly one in ten school students need additional support to meet minimum standards in literacy and numeracy.

Drilling into the data, it is clear that both where a student lives, along with the size of their parents' income, has a huge impact on their educational outcomes. Almost one in three students from poor backgrounds need additional support. The same is true for one in three Indigenous students, one in four students from remote locations and one in two students from very remote locations.

International measures also present a disturbing picture. The Organisation for Economic Cooperation and Development's Programme for International Student Assessment (PISA) gauges our educational progress compared to over 80 other countries. With tests conducted every three years, the 2022 results showed Australian students from disadvantaged backgrounds are far more likely to fall behind in mathematics, science and reading. On average, Australian 15 year olds from the poorest 25 per cent of families read, write and understand mathematics at the level expected of a ten year old, and this gap is growing.[41] Indigenous students are around four years of schooling behind non-Indigenous students.

The PISA results show a decline in our performance. In 2006 Australia ranked sixth in the world in reading; in 2022 we were twelfth. In science we were sixth in the world in 2006; now we are tenth. And in mathematics, we have gone from eighth to sixteenth.

Looking at our trajectories in NAPLAN and PISA, it is clear that our educational performance is deteriorating compared to other countries and that our poorest students are slipping through the cracks. Many of the children who fall behind in primary school never catch up. We see this in classrooms across the nation. Too many university students struggle with foundational literacy and numeracy skills.

To improve as a nation, we need to view higher education as part of the entire learning ecosystem. It is all intertwined.

Speaking at the Universities Australia Solutions Summit in February 2025, Minister Clare summed up the predicament:

> For most of the last decade things have been going in the wrong direction. The number of students finishing school dropped. From 83 per cent to 73 per cent. That's in public schools. Last year, for the first time in about ten years, that percentage went up. A bit. That's a good sign, but there is a long way to go.[42]

Think about that for a second. At a time when we need to compete with the rest of the world and, according to Jobs and Skills Australia, nine out of ten new jobs over the next decade will need post-secondary skills,[43] fewer Australians are completing high school.

To even get close to the Accord's target of 80 per cent of working-age Australians with a tertiary education by 2050, things must change, and fast.

We need to confront the reality that students from low socio-economic and underrepresented groups start one step behind their more affluent peers and may never close the gap.

Nearly one in four teenagers failed to finish Year 12 in 2023, with data from the Australian Curriculum, Assessment and Reporting Authority (ACARA) showing at least 50,000 students left school before Year 12.[44] This was the highest level since 2010. Disturbingly, nearly half of Aboriginal and Torres Strait Islander students left before finishing Year 12, with only 55.8 per cent of Indigenous students matriculating.

The ACARA data is consistent with the minister's observation that 73 per cent of students in government schools finished Year 12 — almost 20 percentage points behind completion rates in private schools (90.4 per cent).

Surely as educators, we must be concerned about this canary in the coalmine. What does it say about equity, fairness and access if the nation's public school students are finishing high school at a much lower rate than those at private schools? Where is the level playing field?

These problems flow onto access to university and limit the opportunities students have for social mobility. For too many, the dream of higher education as a pathway to a more prosperous life is fading. Data from the Australian Centre for Student Equity and Success points to a 10.6 per cent decline in students from low socio-economic backgrounds at university in 2023 compared to 2017.

Over the same period there was also a 15.5 per cent drop in first-in-family students, and a 19.3 per cent drop in students from non-English-speaking backgrounds. Regional and remote students were down 13.9 per cent. On the other hand, the number of students with a disability and the number of Indigenous students has risen.

Too often as a nation we are failing our young people, not just our university students. The system is stacked against the next generation, from the cost of rent and housing to the price of getting an education. Without universities creating education pathways for all students, our national ambition of fairness and greater prosperity falters.

Investing in what economists call our "human capital" and making the most of our talent pool boosts productivity. The Productivity Commission has long argued there are ways to do this, including building a strong early education and school system that delivers foundational skills for all students and boosting incentives for quality teaching in universities and the Vocational Education and Training sector.[45]

We live in a rich, advanced country that fails to fully value the power of education. Collectively, we have created an unfair system that stops many young people getting ahead.

Many of the barriers are financial. Youth Allowance is just $47 a day — or 35 per cent of the minimum wage — while the median rent in Sydney is more than $100 a day. The level of income support is too low for someone studying full-time and living away from home in one of Australia's major cities. The number of students on Youth Allowance has dropped sharply over the past two decades, leading to concerns that poorer students are giving up on university or dropping out due to cost-of-living pressures.[46]

It is not just undergraduate students doing it tough. Postgraduates are also facing real hardship.

Katherine Warwick is a smart and dedicated PhD candidate at Western Sydney University with a passion for water ecology. Her research looks at aquatic ecosystems and contaminates in platypuses. It often involves being knee-deep in water during late-night field trips to monitor platypus populations in eastern New South Wales and the effect that PFOS (perfluorooctane sulfonate) chemical contamination is having on their health.

Yet when Katherine wanders through her local supermarket, she must mentally calculate how many Weet-Bix and how much milk she needs to survive the week. When she gets home she must think twice before turning on the lights due to the cost of electricity.

As a PhD student, she receives $87 a day from a Commonwealth scholarship. Many of our best and brightest postgraduate students are living in poverty, and unsurprisingly PhD enrolments by Australian students fell from 43,174 to 39,801 between 2018 and 2023 — a decline of 8 per cent, despite the population growing by 7 per cent over the same period.

It is imperative that we rethink both Youth Allowance and the PhD stipend if we are to encourage more Australian students into higher education and then on to research that benefits the nation. How can we be a country at the vanguard of knowledge creation, innovation and invention when the very people we need to achieve this cannot make ends meet?

Unpopular in a populist landscape

Decades of declining public funding and flawed incentives have created a financial landscape where universities must generate income to survive, but their fight to survive can run counter to the interests of the students they are meant to serve. Unable to solve this dilemma internally, they have often looked to corporate Australia and consultants for help. The results have been mixed to say the least.

Bringing corporate perspectives into universities *can* be beneficial. Taxpayer funds need to be used efficiently, and universities can learn a lot from parts of the private sector in areas such as human resources, project management and digital services. But any increases in efficiency must support a public purpose, without clouding that mission. This is where many in the community and unions see corporatisation as having got out of hand.

They see universities turning into businesses where generating revenue has become an end in itself, displacing the primary mission of educating students and conducting research. They see a shift of power away from teachers to university management, and the erosion of working conditions as an increasing number of educators are forced into insecure casual employment. And they see universities failing to pay their workforce their full entitlements, with a long list of universities joining an even longer list of private-sector entities that have underpaid their staff.

The result is often a sharp divide between those who run the nation's universities and community sentiment. This is evident in sustained criticism of universities in the media and in national and state inquiries.

In 2024 the University of Tasmania, the only one in the Apple Isle, was the subject of a damning report by the Tasmanian Parliament's Legislative Council Select Committee. The report highlighted problems at the institution, including a "clearly expressed deficit of trust" in the university's governance, management and strategic direction. It stated that:

> the reduction in both numbers and representation on the University Council, and the resulting risk of "group think" was indicated as a cause of diminished accountability and quality in decision-making. The constitution and functioning of the Academic Senate were viewed as being too controlled by executive management. The loss of voice and influence in decision-making by academics at the University, especially on academic matters, in the context of a shift to a more managerial, corporate approach, was a key concern ...[47]

Scathing in its findings, the committee went on to say that "concern was expressed that the university appears to prioritise commercial over community interests in its core functions, with a significant focus on corporatisation which undermines the university's core role and identity".[48]

These findings were about the University of Tasmania, but other universities could equally have found themselves in the political crosshairs. It demonstrates how politicians and the community see things differently from those who run universities. Where the university executive sees their institution as staying true to their purpose, according to YouGov, 54 per cent of Australians think that universities have adopted making a profit as a primary mission.[49]

Another question causing consternation with university governance is the perennial topic of executive pay. Some in the sector see this as a small side issue compared to the larger problems facing universities, but for many in the community it is emblematic of the shift towards corporatisation. One survey found that four in five, or 79 per cent, of Australians agree that vice-chancellor salaries should be capped so they are not paid more than the prime minister.[50]

Dr Alison Barnes, national president of the National Tertiary Education Union, commented on the performance of universities and public perceptions during evidence to a 2025 Senate inquiry into university governance:

> Over 300 senior executives are paid more than state premiers … The average vice-chancellor takes home more than

> $1 million each year. Universities spend up to $730 million in consulting every single year. Sixty-eight per cent of those who are employed in higher education are employed on an insecure basis.[51]

Given the median salary in Australia is around $90,000, it is easy to see how universities are believed to be out of step with public sentiment.[52] The fact that so many university executives are paid more than the politicians who regulate the sector is an ongoing source of friction. Universities are public bodies funded by billions of dollars of taxpayer money. It is reasonable to expect that executive pay reflects the public nature of these bodies, and that salaries are determined in a fair and transparent manner at arm's length from the universities themselves, as occurs for public servants.

At Western Sydney University, we believe the salaries of vice-chancellors should be determined by the independent federal Renumeration Tribunal. This would enable benchmarking against public sector organisations of comparable scale and complexity. That body already sets senior public servant salaries and is well equipped to do the same for universities.

It is a fix for a problem that unnecessarily tarnishes the reputation of the sector.

Misinformation overload

High fees, student dissatisfaction and repeated governance issues dominating the headlines have fuelled an intense political climate for universities. Well before President Donald Trump was re-elected for a second term, the anti-university backlash had taken root both in the United States and here in Australia.

While universities must take responsibility for their failures and eroding social licence, they have also been caught up in crises beyond their control. This includes destabilising changes in government regulation that began with encouraging international student recruitment and ended with limiting this very activity. Universities are also not responsible for the supply-side failures on building new housing, infrastructure bottlenecks and the lack of essential services. Nor did they put in place the lax regulatory policies that saw a host of private education providers emerge only to be deregistered for sharp practices.

Yet, in the land of the tall poppy syndrome, universities have been the perfect scapegoats: perceived as elite, out of touch and, at times, tone deaf to community concerns.

Universities, home to some of the nation's greatest teachers and researchers, have been surprisingly ineffective — and often silent — when it comes to building a coalition of defenders. This leaves the sector vulnerable to government intervention and micromanagement.

In the United States, the higher education environment is highly politicised, not least with regard to the actions being taken against Harvard, America's oldest and wealthiest university. In 2025 President Trump froze $US2.2 billion in federal funding including grants and contracts after Harvard defied demands to change its hiring, admissions and teaching practices. The president has also attempted to block Harvard's ability to enrol international students and threatened its tax-exempt status.

The White House characterises its actions as a crackdown on anti-Semitism. Harvard, which has made extensive changes to address anti-Semitism, frames it as an assault on its independence and constitutional rights. It is suing the Trump administration at the time of writing. In the current climate, Harvard and other institutions are finding it harder to defend their independence.

In Australia, universities have also been subjected to fierce criticism for how they have handled anti-Semitism on their campuses. The prime minister's Special Envoy to Combat Antisemitism, Jillian Segal, has even proposed that universities be defunded should they facilitate, enable or fail to act against anti-Semitism.

There has also been a backlash in the media against Indigenous viewpoints in university courses, particularly Macquarie University's Age and the Law course. Controversy erupted over claims law students were marked on their delivery of an Acknowledgement of Country. The claims and ensuing rhetoric were overblown but demonstrate the "gotcha" public opinion culture that universities face.

Culture wars have long been a hallmark of education systems around the world. Past decades have seen universities at the forefront of heated debates over desegregation, ending the Vietnam War, political correctness and the civil rights movement. What we learn defines who we are. Controlling that flow of information is a source of great power.

Now, more than ever, it is important that we teach critical thinking. Universities and their leaders must champion freedom of speech and the importance of a contest of ideas and instil these values in how we teach our students. If university students are not taken outside their comfort zones, we are missing the mark. Universities should be places of disagreement and challenge at the vanguard of societal battles over freedom of speech, while ensuring zero tolerance for anti-Semitic and Islamophobic hate speech.

Change is constant, but the world in which we live has changed radically in recent years. People view — and value — knowledge differently. The availability of knowledge has also radically altered. Rather than being scarce and often limited to universities, it is ubiquitous and free thanks to the internet and generative AI systems such as ChatGPT. Expert medical, legal, mathematical and other information is now only a prompt away.

Generative AI can produce content that challenges the role of academics. In my field of constitutional law, I asked ChatGPT to draft a question for a 2,000-word essay on bills of rights for second-year public law students. The tool came up with an excellent question that needed no editing. I then asked it to provide a sample answer and mark it according to a predetermined marking guide. ChatGPT completed each step with ease and awarded itself a high distinction! I would have given it the same mark as an essay produced by one of my very best students.

This is only the beginning of generative AI's capabilities, which will increase exponentially over the coming years. The fact that it is already able to replicate the work of academics and students at a high level illustrates the need for a fundamental rethink.

We must move away from a focus on the transmission of knowledge and instead concentrate on skills such as critical analysis and creativity where humans can add value to generative AI systems. In the case of my essay for public law students, it might mean asking students to produce a first draft with AI (to test their understanding of how to use the system) and then assessing them on their ability to critique the draft for errors and algorithmic bias, and to produce a refined draft based on their insights.

Social media has transformed perceptions of who holds knowledge and who can disseminate their opinions, the result of which is increasing scepticism of expertise and rational thinking. It is no coincidence that the erosion of trust and confidence in our universities is replicated in a loss of faith in other important public institutions.

One example is the 2023 referendum on an Indigenous Voice to Parliament that saw significant social media engagement coupled with hashtags making allegations of rigging such as #StopTheSteal and #RiggedReferendum. This American-style election conspiracy-building even attacked the Australian Election Commission, despite its long and proud record of impartially and fairly conducting such votes.

In *People Power: How Australian referendums are lost and won*, David Hume and I wrote how we cannot let attacks on the integrity of our voting system become entrenched.[53] Yet our current system is designed in a way that produces misinformation and polarisation, leading to community confusion and anxiety. Since the referendum, the scales have become even more unbalanced.

We have never known a time where facts themselves are so greatly disputed, and disinformation is rife. Knowledge is in competition with misinformation, disinformation and social media, and too often knowledge is losing out. These broader forces challenge the role of universities and their focus on evidence and rational debate.

Universities cannot abdicate the field and allow misinformation and disinformation to proliferate. If opinions are being formed and ideas tested online, universities must be there too.

Stepping out of our comfort zone

Soon after I started as vice-chancellor of Western Sydney University in 2024, I convened an online webinar for our staff to hear from them, answer their questions, and start developing a new strategy for the future of Western. The webinar attracted over a thousand people and was a spirited session. I then convened a similar event for our 50,000 students and the numbers were paltry, with only 25 turning up.

Our students had sent us a clear message. We had to pivot to adopt their medium of communication, and this meant social media. We set up Instagram and TikTok live sessions that attracted over a thousand students. Student engagement was lively, with a lot of humour and great questions. It demonstrated the importance of engaging with our students in a space where they were happy to share their stories, including their struggles to afford food and their distress at the cost of their degrees.

Interacting with our students on their terms is something I do as often as I can. I joke I am the first vice-chancellor in Australia on TikTok. This has taken me well out of my comfort zone, including having to do a headstand when I lost a bet. Social media is not an easy place for me, but for our students it is their civic space.

My presence on social media also forges connections that might otherwise prove difficult. I have had many students come up to say hello after recognising me as "that guy from TikTok". Some then ask what I do at the University. They may not know me as their vice-chancellor (or even what a vice-chancellor is — something from *Star Wars* perhaps?), but social media has proved a great way to bridge the gap and start a conversation.

Where once information was shared in the town square, via the printing press, radio, television and newspapers, for today's younger generation it is social media. If we vacate that space as educators, we cede the ground to populism and debates that are not grounded in facts, rationality or expertise. We need to meet this challenge to the role of universities head-on.

We must look to build trust and social licence from the inside out. This means being present in places like social media where information is shared, and our community discusses the questions that concern them. We must either adapt to new technologies and modes of communication or lose relevance.

We must also break down barriers. There is a reason that for many people universities evoke images of walls or impenetrable fortresses. Once this was as a protector and incubator of knowledge, but in a society where gratification is immediate and self-appointed experts are on every screen, it makes universities seem out of touch. It is not enough for us to make higher education more accessible and relatable; we must also leave the fortress. We must go to where our students and the community are and we must listen on their terms.

Universities are not used to doing things this way. It is disconcerting for a sector used to being the experts and keepers of knowledge. We need to change.

Sidestepping the Kodak moment

As universities become more regulated and face increasing change, they must also contend with technological disruption. Online learning was well advanced before the COVID-19 pandemic and, coupled with rapid developments in generative AI, the threat of a "Kodak moment" looms ever present.

Universities must self-disrupt before we are overtaken by private entities better able to deliver higher education in the new digital landscape. It is far from fanciful that soon we will see something like a Netflix for higher education: a global platform offering low-cost qualifications with excellent employment opportunities. In such a world, people will rightly ask: why do I need a degree from a university when my learning can be certified by a reputable global company at a fraction of the cost?

In fact, that future is already here. One example is the American Coursera website, which partners with universities and industry leaders to deliver online courses. It is now a direct competitor to Australian universities in offering qualifications ranging from short courses to professional certificates and even full degrees. Coursera incorporates educational programs by some of the world's largest companies. Google Career Certificates in areas such as data analytics, cybersecurity or project management take up to ten hours per week over three to six months and have attracted millions of learners. The cost? $90 per month.

Universities must respond by embracing the need for fundamental changes to how and what we teach, including personalising our offerings so that they align with the needs and preferences of our students. Western Sydney University Chancellor, Professor Jennifer Westacott AC, points out disruption in our society is challenging antiquated and traditional education models. She believes universities must disrupt and lead, particularly with regard to "the outdated academic structure which goes against what students want — which is choice and flexibility".[54]

It is imperative in doing so that universities remain public bastions of knowledge, critical thought and freedom of expression. Universities need to fight for this, knowing that success is not guaranteed. The cohesiveness, tolerance and progressive nature of our society depends on a strong higher education sector.

Technological change also means the role of universities is evolving — we must not only prepare students with the skills they need in a digital society; we need to prepare them for jobs that do not yet exist. Many students will start a three- or five-year degree program only to find that a new set of opportunities has emerged during their studies. People need a degree that serves them through life changes, not a new degree each time they get a job.

This highlights the importance of soft skills such as communication, critical thinking and the ability to work in teams. These skills are the building blocks of resilience and adaptability. Today's and tomorrow's graduates won't work the same job over a lifetime; they'll be constantly reskilling and upskilling in professional and vocational employment.

In the World Economic Forum's *Future of Jobs Report (2023)*, employers estimated that 44 per cent of workers' skills will be disrupted over the next five years. Cognitive skills are growing in importance most quickly, which reflects the demand placed on people who are able to undertake complex problem solving. Creative thinking ranked slightly above analytical thinking, while technological literacy was the third fastest growing core skill.[55]

In 2024 Jobs and Skills Australia research showed that societal and technological change will mean that over 90 per cent of employment growth over the next ten years will be in jobs that require post-secondary qualifications, with half being university-qualified roles. They identified 37 emerging roles across four key themes, including health (due to our ageing population), and technological, digital and environmental change.[56]

While job ads for quantum computing scientists are still fairly low with 55 listings in 2022, over the five years prior there was an almost 700 per cent increase in demand. Unsurprisingly, roles centred around Australia's commitment to reach net zero emissions by 2050 are also increasingly popular, including electric vehicle technicians and sustainability consultants.

In 2022 the Tech Council of Australia estimated the nation will need to employ an additional 186,000 people in order to meet the nation's tech jobs target,[57] while in 2023 Engineers Australia predicted a shortfall of up to 100,000 engineers.[58] We have 4,000 fewer teachers than we need, and the nation is likely to be short of 123,000 nurses by 2030.[59]

At Western Sydney University our ambition is for every student to not just be digitally proficient but to be a digital leader. Our students in every field need to be equipped to use technology, be adept at asking critical questions about the outputs of generative AI, and to be able to identify algorithmic bias.

Artificial intelligence is here to stay, and it will redefine employment. It has enormous potential to facilitate better, more efficient ways of working. As educators, our role is to embrace the opportunities and guide the rollout of this technology in ethical ways. It is also to ensure our students graduate with the power of critical thinking.

Universities must champion people thinking for themselves. It is why arts and humanities — currently the most expensive degrees — are needed more than ever. We need more creative thinkers in fields like philosophy, history and literature to interpret and understand our rapidly changing world. Now is a dangerous time for universities to pigeonhole their students in vocational programs. Instead, we must broaden the horizons of every student by exposing them to new and often uncomfortable ideas and prepare them to thrive during disruptive change.

What needs to be done?

Universities are not victims, nor are they powerless. Our alumni can be counted in the millions, and much of the future success of our nation will be driven by higher education. Without universities producing graduates with cutting-edge skills in areas such as AI, and without their research enabling new discoveries and innovations, the productivity gains and improvements in living standards sought by the Albanese government will be impossible to attain.

It is time for universities to rediscover their mission and voice as public institutions operating for the public good. To achieve this, we must listen to our students and the community with humility, and act to address the problems eating away at the foundations of our sector and our society. Universities are being undermined by inequality but are one of the best solutions to this.

Australia's future depends on resolving this dilemma. If universities falter, a generation of Australians will fail to achieve their potential. Disillusionment and disappointment will set in. The nation will be at risk of becoming more socially fragmented, less prosperous, and less agile and adaptable in the face of technological, geopolitical and demographic change. People will be in danger of losing their ability to question and to think critically, becoming more susceptible to misinformation and disinformation. Such a scenario would further test the strength and cohesiveness of our democracy. One only has to look to the United States to see how this might play out.

Government and universities must urgently act to repair Australia's higher education system. A good place for the government to start is to charge students fair and reasonable fees. The JRG package introduced in 2021 has failed in its attempt to use price signals to steer students away from the arts and humanities. It has also undermined the funding model needed by universities to support Australian students.

The government must revisit its policy on international student limits, which are wreaking havoc across the sector. The policy was always misdirected with the claim that it was about housing and neglected the fact that international students are contributors to Australia. They generate economic activity and jobs, fill critical skill shortages, and build long-term goodwill for the nation around the world.

International student caps harm Australians. In the absence of additional government investment, the income these students provide supports thousands of local jobs and subsidises critical services like food pantries and community dinners for our Australian students who might otherwise go hungry. Without extra government funding, universities are left with tough choices as to which jobs must go and what services must be wound back.

The government has begun to repair the damage by announcing an extra 25,000 international student places for 2026, 17,500 of which are for publicly funded universities. Places will be allocated to universities engaged in Southeast Asia with adequate student accommodation. This is a welcome sign. The challenge will be attracting students from that region when other government actions — such as the increased non-refundable visa fee — act as a disincentive for them to study here.

While the government has yet to dismantle the JRG, it is developing new funding systems for universities. These include a Managed Growth Funding System that will more tightly administer domestic enrolments, and Needs-based Funding that will provide additional money for students requiring support, including those from Indigenous and low socio-economic backgrounds. These measures are promising, but their effect will be limited without a significant injection of government funds. If the government does not make up the lost revenue from international students and the decline in funding for Australian students, many universities will remain mired in a cycle of cost-cutting and job losses.

These and other changes could be achieved by recommitting to the ambition of the Accord. That document emerged from an exhaustive, nationwide consultation process that outlined a vision for the sector for the coming decades. It recognised that our future prosperity depends on highly skilled Australians able to thrive in a competitive international environment.

The Accord called for the proportion of working people with a post-school qualification to increase from 60 per cent to 80 per cent by 2050. This requires more people from low socio-economic, first-in-family, Indigenous and regional and rural backgrounds to enrol and succeed at university. The system is not geared to achieve this and is stacked against students from poorer backgrounds. The Accord recognises this and provides a much-needed blueprint for reform that puts students first.

Universities also need to lead change. We are not just facing a reputational crisis; we are facing a challenge to our legitimacy. It is a defining moment in our long history. With our social licence under threat, we must genuinely acknowledge where we have made mistakes and take corrective action. This must be true to our purpose of being institutions that educate students first and foremost and set them on a path for a better life. Students — not dollars and rankings — need to drive decision-making.

Universities must get better at telling their stories about how they are fulfilling this purpose. At Western Sydney University, we are proud to celebrate our alumni and their achievements. People like Winnie Dunn, who was nominated for the Miles Franklin Literary Award for her novel, *Dirt Poor Islanders*, the first ever Tongan Australian novel published. Or our student-led solar car team that took on the world in the 2025 Bridgestone World Solar Challenge from Darwin to Adelaide. Or newly minted District Court judge, Imad Abdul-Karim, who arrived in Australia as a refugee from Lebanon at age 15 and graduated in 1998 as part of our first School of Law cohort. Or our humanitarian initiatives like the People Fleeing Conflict scholarship program which is giving refugees like Roua Elbashety hope and a second chance at life and an education. With Western's support, Roua, who is a Palestinian from Gaza, is one step closer to her dream of becoming a nurse.

At our autumn graduation ceremonies in 2025, for the first time in our history we had two Indigenous people officiate: Deputy Vice-Chancellor, Indigenous Leadership, Professor Michelle Trudgett; and Pro Vice-Chancellor, Indigenous Education, Professor Susan Page. Michelle described it as "breaking down the walls of institutions which have for many decades excluded Indigenous people, one ceremony at a time".

It is watershed moments like these that we must champion and share. They remind us that we must be tethered to our purpose and our role as public sector entities delivering public good.

The room was silent when the Chancellor of the University of Technology Sydney, Professor Catherine Livingstone AC, delivered her address to the 2025 Universities Australia conference in Canberra. Summing up the issues confronting the sector, Professor Livingstone said that public concerns about university operations had led to questions over governance:

> We were perceived to be too slow to react to specific issues, and on occasions even in denial, and to be out of step with broader concerns about efficiency and effectiveness of the use of resources ... So, inevitably, this led to concerns being raised about the governance of universities. Interestingly, for

> a sector that's funded with significant public money, there is more reference to global aspirations and rankings than there is to the contribution of Australia's prosperity and wellbeing. Continuing to assert our value in generic terms around student and research outcomes, coupled with entitled demands for money, is not serving to engage the trust of our key stakeholders — quite the opposite in fact.[60]

Canberra University Vice-Chancellor Bill Shorten argued in *The Australian* that the incoming generation of students sees a disconnect between an outdated version of an Australian university and themselves:

> Too often millennials and Gen Z look at universities and see cold institutions that talk about themselves; obsessing over prestige or over rankings that give no indication of what is behind the curtain, of what the day-to-day experience is actually like. That information is critical to their choice, because what

> it is actually like has a lot of money, time and personal sacrifice riding on it.
>
> These young people do not want the overwhelming array of product information, in inaccessible forms and vocabulary. Nor the images of students — all aspirational and middle class — that simply don't reflect how members of this new generation see themselves. They want a university that values and encourages a learning community, not a slick and soulless corporation that sees everything through the lens of revenue.[61]

It is exactly why, above all, universities need to return students to the centre of everything we do. We need to care for our people and build trust through transparency and consistency. We need to step back, listen and then act. We need to forge meaningful and mutually beneficial partnerships with our students, our staff, industry and our community. And we need to demonstrate the value in universities, and the value in getting a degree.

At Western, this is what we spend every day striving to achieve.

Dollars are not our bottom line; it is seeing our students receive their degrees at graduation. Two-thirds of our students are the first in their family to attend university, and many are the first in their family to finish high school.

We have the highest number of students from low socio-economic and non-English-speaking backgrounds of any Australian university. Many arrive as refugees or from disadvantaged backgrounds, carrying with them stories of resilience, ambition and hope. Their presence on our campuses is a daily reminder of the transformative power of education. When our students succeed, the effects ripple far beyond our region, reaching families and communities around the world.

The most impactful moments in my tenure as a vice-chancellor have been with students. It might have been teaching a class at our Justice Clinic, serving food at a community dinner in Campbelltown, or handing out rice and oats at our Food Pantry. I have been privileged to hear their stories, including one paramedicine student living in their car because they could not afford accommodation, or an international student grateful for the dinner as an opportunity to make a friend.

I have learnt from spending time in our Student Services Hub. Students came through our doors with questions, and I listened as we answered their queries. It opened my eyes to the barriers and hardships they face. Too often universities themselves are the problem by making study too complex and imposing barriers through systems that can test the patience of a saint. Instead, universities need to be designed around the needs of their students.

I have also learnt a lot from my time on TikTok. I thought I understood the needs and preferences of students today, but my understanding was based on what university was like in the 1980s and 90s. Too often, people such as myself interpret the needs of students through how we saw the world as students ourselves.

Students today are facing a different set of pressures and problems, including a wide digital divide that means many cannot afford internet access at home, or even a laptop. Many undertake their studies with nothing better than a mobile phone, which is hardly the device needed to write a 3,000-word essay.

I truly believe that no region in Australia has greater potential than Western Sydney, and no university has a greater responsibility to ensure the community can get ahead. We are driven to change the trajectory for entire generations, opening up new possibilities by being relevant, accessible and a constant presence in local communities. Education changes lives: it is the ticket to a better life and prosperity for individuals, families and regions.

Universities face financial challenges driven by factors such as international student caps, shifting student demand and cost-of-living pressures. At Western, like so many in the sector, we are not immune to these headwinds. Our revenue has been hit hard, and we have to live within our means, which means cutting services, and good people losing their jobs.

While we rein in costs in the short term, we are also delivering on a bright, longer-term future by resetting our university to focus on our core job of teaching and research. Everything we do needs to be through the lens of students first.

On top of ensuring the digital prowess of our

students, our ambition is to ensure every student has the opportunity for industry experience through on-the-job training, internships, placements and work experience. These programs — like degree apprenticeships — are designed to provide a direct pathway to employment or a job that begins while students are still studying with us. It is about building deeper connections with the people, industries and communities around us and dismantling barriers.

Universities must also be better workplaces. We need to improve how we care for our people, which after all is the best way of ensuring they perform at their best. It is hard for academics to be great teachers or to plan their curriculum for the longer term, let alone to build a fulfilling career, if they do not know whether they will be employed from one semester to the next. There are too many examples of universities letting their staff down, whether it be through underpaying salaries or over-relying on insecure work.

Fostering a culture of inclusion and genuine engagement with staff based on a commitment to intellectual freedom can be another focus. A successful university means staff embracing the opportunity to contribute to the collective public mission of the institution, while finding room for a diversity of views and strong disagreement. People must be able to challenge management and explore uncomfortable ideas in their teaching and research. This requires a feeling of safety and security at work, which sadly has been absent in many academic workplaces.

In June 2025 our unwavering commitment to our mission — student success, impactful research and stronger communities — saw Western Sydney University pull off a remarkable feat. For the fourth year in a row, we topped the global Times Higher Education Impact Rankings.

There are many university rankings. This one is different. Rather than measuring reputation, academic citations or research income, the Impact Rankings assess what universities are doing to improve lives by delivering the United Nations Sustainable Development Goals. These 17 goals outline the world's biggest challenges, including ending poverty, providing affordable and clean energy, reducing inequality, fostering industry innovation and producing sustainable cities and communities. These measures describe the future and planet we want for our generation and those to come. The ranking assesses real-world impact in achieving these goals across more than 2500 universities from 130 countries. I am proud of what we have achieved, but there is so much more to do.

During Welcome Week, I dubbed 2025 the year of the student. As I reflect on the journey ahead, the reality is that every year needs to be the year of the student. It is why we exist, and it must be front and centre of everything we do.

All of us across the higher education sector must not only prepare our students for the future, we must help shape the world they will inherit. To achieve this, we need to drive the evolution of universities for a new generation while remaining true to our values and purpose. And we must fulfil our mission to serve the public good by delivering fairness and opportunity in higher education to all.

Endnotes

1 Barker (2025) "'A kind of monster': why does everyone hate universities?", https://www.smh.com.au/national/a-kind-of-monster-why-does-everyone-hate-universities-20250626-p5mann.html

2 Price (2025) "Don't go to university next year. Just don't", https://www.smh.com.au/national/don-t-go-to-university-next-year-just-don-t-20250707-p5md7c.html

3 Grundy (2025) "Polling – Higher Education", https://australiainstitute.org.au/report/polling-higher-education/

4 JWS Research, Benchmark and evaluation research (2024), prepared for Universities Australia

5 Jones (2025) "U.S. Confidence in Higher Education Now Closely Divided", https://news.gallup.com/poll/646880/confidence-highereducation-closelydivided.aspx

6 Quiggin (2025) Submission 11 to the Quality of governance at Australian higher education providers, Senate Standing Committees on Education and Employment

7 Littleton (2023) "Public Attitudes on Issues in Higher Education", https://australiainstitute.org.au/wp-content/uploads/2023/07/

Public-attitudes-on-education-FINAL.pdf

8 Turner (2025) *Broken: Universities, Politics and the Public Good*, Monash University Publishing, p 2

9 Norton (2023) "Tumult and transformation: the story of Australian universities over the past 30 years", https://theconversation.com/tumult-and-transformation-the-story-of-australian-universities-over-the-past-30-years-215536

10 Ey (2021) "The Higher Education Loan Program (HELP) and related loans: a chronology", https://www.aph.gov.au/About_Parliament/Parliamentary_departments/Parliamentary_Library/Research/Chronologies/2020-21/HigherEducation

11 Norton (2023)

12 Turner (2025) p 4

13 Sharrock (2013) "Book review: *The Dawkins Revolution, 25 Years On*", https://theconversation.com/book-review-the-dawkins-revolution-25-years-on-19291

14 Norton (2019) "Why Australia should revert to demand-driven funding of universities", https://grattan.edu.au/news/why-australia-should-revert-to-demand-driven-funding-of-universities/

15 Norton (2019) "Demand-driven funding for universities is frozen. What does this mean and should the policy be restored?", https://theconversation.com/demand-driven-funding-for-universities-is-frozen-what-does-this-mean-and-should-the-policy-be-restored-116060

16 Kabatek (2023) "Only 1.5% of students swapped fields due to the 'Job-ready Graduates' fee changes", https://findanexpert.unimelb.edu.au/news/68926-only-1.5-of-students-swapped-fields-

due-to-the-'job-ready-graduates'-fee-changes

17 Thrower (2024) "University is expensive. Impacts of rising university costs on young people", https://australiainstitute.org.au/wp-content/uploads/2024/11/P1736-University-is-expensive-Web-1.pdf

18 Grundy (2025)

19 Australian Taxation Office (2024) "Revenue Collection 2023–2024. Higher Education Loan Program (HELP) and Student Financial Supplement Scheme (SFSS) collections", https://www.transparency.gov.au/publications/treasury/australian-taxation-office/australian-taxation-office-annual-report-2023-24/part-4-%E2%80%93-revenue-performance/revenue-collection

20 Universities Admission Centre (2025) "Student Lifestyle and Learning Report 2025", https://www.uac.edu.au/submissions-and-reports/student-lifestyle-and-learning-report-2025

21 Thrower (2024)

22 Duffy (2025) "Graduates in 'debt vortex' as HECS front and centre for first time in an election", https://www.abc.net.au/news/2025-04-16/federal-election-2025-hecs-student-debt-policies/105177248

23 Turner (2025) p 10

24 Productivity Commission (2023) "5-year Productivity Inquiry: From learning to growth. Inquiry report – volume 8", https://www.pc.gov.au/inquiries/completed/productivity/report/productivity-volume8-education-skills.pdf

25 Clare (2022) "Universities Accord", https://ministers.education.gov.au/clare/universities-accord

26 Turner (2025) p 9

27 Turner (2025) pp 9–10

28 Universities Australia (2025) "Productivity inquiries – response", https://universitiesaustralia.edu.au/wp-content/uploads/2025/06/Productivity-inquiries-response-Universities-Australia.pdf p3

29 Read (2024) "Foreign students are saving the economy", https://www.afr.com/policy/economy/foreign-students-are-saving-the-economy-20240308-p5fasz

30 Department of Education (nd) "Education export income – Calendar year", https://www.education.gov.au/international-education-data-and-research/education-export-income-calendar-year

31 Moore (2023) "Invested: Australia's Southeast Asia Economic Strategy to 2040", https://www.dfat.gov.au/sites/default/files/invested-southeast-asia-economic-strategy-2040.pdf, p 85

32 Chrysanthos (2024) "Dutton calls overstaying international students 'the modern version of boat arrivals'", https://www.smh.com.au/politics/federal/dutton-calls-overstaying-international-students-the-modern-version-of-boat-arrivals-20240926-p5kdrw.html

33 Bita (2025) "Universities warned over foreign students and cyber threats", https://www.theaustralian.com.au/education/universities-warned-over-foreign-students-and-cyber-threats/news-story/5531578fd43ddfae631c3363653db47c

34 Universities Australia (2025) "2025–26 Pre-budget submission", https://universitiesaustralia.edu.au/wp-content/uploads/2025/02/2025-26-Pre-budget-submission-1.pdf

35 Littleton (2023) p 14

36 Turner (2025) p 11

37 Ross (2025) "Australian universities' per-student teaching costs soar by fifth", https://www.timeshighereducation.com/news/australian-universities-student-teaching-costs-soar-fifth
38 KordaMentha (2024) "Higher Education Annual Report", https://kordamentha.com/2024-kordamentha-higher-education-annual-report, p 4
39 Student Experience Survey (2023) "2023 Results", https://www.qilt.edu.au/surveys/student-experience-survey-(ses)
40 Winkler (2025) "Fresh insights into domestic student demand", https://futurecampus.com.au/2025/07/13/fresh-insights-into-domestic-student-demand/
41 Clare (2023) "New report highlights importance of the next National School Reform Agreement", https://ministers.education.gov.au/clare/new-report-highlights-importance-next-national-school-reform-agreement; https://www.theaustralian.com.au/nation/school-system-fails-fairness-test-as-pisa-results-show-learning-gap/news-story/d2279ebf2a59f73ff9f38b9decf6269f
42 Clare (2025) "Universities Australia Solutions Summit", https://ministers.education.gov.au/clare/universities-australia-solutions-summit
43 Jobs and Skills Australia (2023) "Employment projections for the decade ahead", https://www.jobsandskills.gov.au/publications/towards-national-jobs-and-skills-roadmap-summary/employment-projections-for-the-decade-ahead
44 Bita (2024) "One in four students are failing to finish high school", https://www.theaustralian.com.au/nation/

one-in-four-students-are-failing-to-finish-high-school/news-story/5aef611476816717999ef1a522b481bc

45 Wood (2024) "The fraying generational bargain", https://www.pc.gov.au/media-speeches/speeches/generational-bargain/generational-bargain.pdf

46 Medhora (2025) "Number of students on Youth Allowance drops significantly in 20 years", https://www.abc.net.au/news/2025-07-01/youth-allowance-numbers-drop-significantly/105479342

47 Parliament of Tasmania (2024) "Legislative Council Select Committee Final Report on the Provisions of the University of Tasmania Act 1992", https://www.parliament.tas.gov.au/__data/assets/pdf_file/0026/88721/LCSC-UTAS-Act-Final-Report-23-December-2024.pdf, p 4

48 Parliament of Tasmania (2024) "Legislative Council Select Committee Final Report on The Provisions of the University of Tasmania Act 1992", p 20

49 Grundy (2025)

50 Littleton (2023) p 1

51 Hansard, Commonwealth of Australia (2025) "Senate Education and Employment Legislation Committee, Quality of Governance at Australian higher education providers", https://www.aph.gov.au/Parliamentary_Business/Hansard/Hansard_Display?bid=committees/commsen/28764/&sid=0001#:~:text=Over%20300%20senior%20executives%20are,employed%20on%20an%20insecure%20basis

52 Australian Bureau of Statistics (2025) "Average Weekly Earnings, Australia", https://www.abs.gov.au/

statistics/labour/earnings-and-working-conditions/average-weekly-earnings-australia/nov-2024

53 Hume, Williams (2024) *People Power: How Australian referendums are lost and won*, UNSW Press

54 Westacott (2025) "Western Sydney University 35th anniversary speech", https://www.westernsydney.edu.au/newscentre/news_centre/more_news_stories/35th_anniversary_speech_chancellor_professor_jennifer_westacott_ao

55 World Economic Forum (2023) "Future of Jobs Report 2023", https://www3.weforum.org/docs/WEF_Future_of_Jobs_2023.pdf, p 7

56 Jobs and Skills Australia (2024) "Emerging Roles", https://www.jobsandskills.gov.au/research/emerging-roles

57 Tech Council of Australia (2022) "The Plan To Realise Goal Of Having 1.2 Million Tech Workers In Australia By 2030", https://techcouncil.com.au/newsroom/getting-to-1-2million/

58 Engineers Australia (2023) *The engineering profession: a statistical overview, 15th edition*, https://www.engineersaustralia.org.au/news-and-media/2023/12/new-report-reveals-deepening-engineering-skills-crisis

59 Sheehy (2025) "Universities Australia. Unimutual Conference, keynote address", https://universitiesaustralia.edu.au/media-item/keynote-address-unimutual-conference-adelaide-south-australia/

60 Bita (2025) "Diversion ahead: universities demand roads funding", https://www.theaustralian.com.

au/higher-education/business-veteran-catherine-livingstone-tells-universities-they-have-a-tin-ear-to-public-concerns-over-funding-and-housing/news-story/60f38a3aae2a61d529efb4a868c9f972

61 Shorten (2025) "Post-pandemic universities need to build communities, not ivory towers", https://www.theaustralian.com.au/commentary/postpandemic-universities-need-to-build-communities-not-ivory-towers/news-story/46f9894892fcaaf1f1510c545ccc aaa8

Acknowledgements

This essay owes an enormous debt to Stefanie Balogh for her drafting, research and general all-round brilliance. Thanks also to the people who so generously commented on earlier drafts: Emma Armson, Richard Denniss, Clare Field and Jennifer Westacott.

About the author

George Williams is the Vice-Chancellor and President of Western Sydney University. He previously served as Deputy Vice-Chancellor, Dean of Law and Anthony Mason Professor at the University of New South Wales. He is a leading constitutional lawyer, co-author with Professor Megan Davis of *Everything You Need to Know about the Voice* and author and editor of dozens more books. He has appeared as a barrister in the High Court and led major public inquiries.

About The Australia Institute

The Australia Institute conducts research that drives the public debate and secures policy outcomes to make Australia better.

The Australia Institute's independence and nonpartisanship ensure our work is guided by a vision for a fairer Australia, without political or commercial influence. Our research regularly calls into question powerful vested interests, multinational corporations, and the economic orthodoxy.

This work is only possible because of independent donations. The support of our donors powers the Institute's ability to fulfil its motto: research that matters. To contribute to our work and ongoing research, you can make a donation on our website by scanning the QR code below.

Vantage Point Issue 2

Dead Centre: How political pragmatism is killing us
Richard Denniss
August 2025

The sensible centre. Evidence-based policy. These are not the same. In fact, they are at odds with each other.

The scientific evidence tells us that building new gas, oil and coal mines will cause catastrophic climate damage this century. Yet politicians describe a call for the end of new mines as extreme. Likewise with online gambling, junk food advertising or incarcerating children: the evidence of harm is clear, but the sensible centre is defined not by evidence but by politics. Media reports on such issues presuppose that there are two sides and a centre to every debate, but evidence shows there is not. The political right thrives in such fear-fuelled, fact-free arenas, where traditional media and subject matter experts struggle to fight fear with facts.

In this essay, economist and Executive Director of The Australia Institute, Richard Denniss, explores the contradiction between centrism and evidence that sits at the heart of democratic debate in Australia. He shows that when both major parties oppose reform then the position of the sensible centre becomes indistinguishable from blind support for keeping things as they are.

Vantage Point Issue 4

What We Owe the Water:
It's time for a Fossil Fuel Treaty
Kumi Naidoo

"From the flood-soaked streets of Lismore to the rising waters in the Pacific, the effects of climate change are here. Australia stands at a profound crossroads. It can continue to fuel the climate crisis as one of the world's largest fossil fuel exporters or it can become a true partner to its Pacific neighbours and lead the transition towards a fossil-free future."

Genuine solidarity means more than symbolic gestures on the global stage. It means concrete action: ending the approval of new fossil fuel projects and supporting governments seeking to negotiate a Fossil Fuel Non-Proliferation Treaty.

Become a subscriber

- Receive four thought-provoking essays from leading experts each year
- Short enough to read in one or two sittings, long enough for in-depth analysis
- Free postage within Australia

Australia Institute Press

DOLLARS & SENSE

with Greg Jericho

The Australia Institute
Research that matters

Vantage Point Issue 3

Read it and pass it on. Put your name and email below and start a conversation with other readers.

Name	Contact